Cool Cars

Mary Kate Doman

Enslow Elementary

an imprint of

Enslow Publishers, Inc.
40 Industrial Road
Box 398
Berkeley Heights, NJ 07922
USA

http://www.enslow.com

For Liam, who loves things that go.

Enslow Elementary, an imprint of Enslow Publishers, Inc.

Enslow Elementary® is a registered trademark of Enslow Publishers, Inc.

Library of Congress Cataloging-in-Publication Data

Doman, Mary Kate, 1979–
    Cool cars / by Mary Kate Doman.
        p. cm. — (All about big machines)
    Includes index.
    Summary: "Learn about cool cars"—Provided by publisher.
    ISBN 978-0-7660-3930-8
    1. Automobiles—Juvenile literature. I. Title.
    TL147.D657 2012
    629.222—dc23

                                    2011014637

Paperback ISBN 978-1-59845-242-6

Printed in the United States of America

072015 Bang Printing, Brainerd, MN

10 9 8 7 6 5 4 3 2

To Our Readers: We have done our best to make sure all Internet Addresses in this book were active and appropriate when we went to press. However, the author and the publisher have no control over and assume no liability for the material available on those Internet sites or on other Web sites they may link to. Any comments or suggestions can be sent by e-mail to comments@enslow.com or to the address on the back cover.

Photo Credits: © 2011 Photos.com, a division of Getty Images. All rights reserved., pp. title page, 8–9; 14–15, 18–19, 20–21; Fedor Selivanov/Shutterstock.com, pp. 16–17; gary718/Shutterstock.com, p. 6; L Barnwell/Shutterstock.com, p. 12(top); Luis Louro/Shutterstock.com, pp. 22–23; Mikhail/ Shutterstock. com, pp. 10–11; Shutterstock.com, p. 12 (bottom); Stanislaw Tokarski/Shutterstock.com, p. 4.

Cover Photo: Mikhail/Shutterstock.com

Note to Parents and Teachers

Help pre-readers get a jumpstart on reading. These lively stories introduce simple concepts with repetition of words and short simple sentences. Photos and illustrations fill the pages with color and effectively enhance the text. Free Educator Guides are available for this series at www.enslow.com. Search for the *All About Big Machines* series name.

Contents

Words to Know

  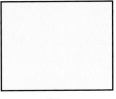

car   purple   yellow

Some cool cars are old.

Some cool cars are new.

Some cool cars are red.

9

Some cool cars are yellow.

Some cool cars are blue and purple.

Some cool cars are big.

Some cool cars are small.

Some cool cars go fast.

Some cool cars go slow.

But all cool cars go, go, go!

Read More

Sutton, Richard. *Car.* New York: DK Publishing, Inc. 2005.

Gould, Robert. *Monster Trucks.* Carlsbad, CA: Big Guy Books, 2004.

Salas, Laura Purdie. *Z is for Zoom: A Race Car Alphabet.* Mankato, Minn.: Capstone Press, 2010.

Web Sites

Monster Cars
<http://www.monsterjam.com/KidsZone/>

Remarkable Cars
<www.remarkablecars.com>

Index

Guided Reading Level: C
Guided Reading Leveling System is based on the guidelines recommended by Fountas and Pinnell.

Word Count: 53